Putting the Broken Pieces of My Life Together

KLRPUBLISHING

Putting the Broken Pieces of My Life Together is a non-fiction book.
Copyright 2021 by Katrina Lynnette Royster
ISBN: 978-0-578-37995-1

All rights reserved. No part of this publication may be reproduced, stored in a retrieval system, or transmitted in any form or by any means—for example, electronic, photocopy, and recording—without the prior written permission of the publisher. The only exception is brief quotations in printed reviews.

Scriptures noted NIV are taken from the Holy Bible, New International Version®, NIV® Copyright ©1973, 1978, 1984, 2011 by Biblica, Inc.® Used by permission. All rights reserved worldwide.
Free Yourself from Painful Memories, Reclaiming Your Inner Child,
copy write ©, 1993 by Ken Parker
Scriptures noted KJV are taken from the Holy Bible, King James version, public domain.
Scriptures noted NKJV are taken from the New King James Version®.
Copyright © 1982 by Thomas Nelson. Used by permission. All rights reserved.
Published by KLR Publishing in the United States by Ingram Books
Edited by Linda Stubblefield, Affordable Christian Editing
Cover Design by Janae Matthews
Back Cover Photo by Nhu Photography
Interior Design by Janae Matthews
Library of Congress Control Number: 1-11093786621
ISBN: 978-0-578-37995-1 (paper book)

*"God wants us to share our pain so that
He can redeem our pain by healing other people."*
— *Author Unknown* —

Putting the Broken Pieces of My Life Together

BY KATRINA LYNNETTE ROYSTER

Dedication

I dedicate this book to Jesus Christ my Savior, who though He was God, He came to earth as a man to save me. Without Him, this book would not be possible. To my children, Joshua, Jordan, Janae, Joy and Leah, the wonderful adults in my life. I love you, and I thank God for you. To my mother, I love you, I thank you for taking care of me to the best of your ability and strength. I thank you for allowing me to live. To my grandmother and grandfather, I thank you for raising me and instilling within me the foundation for survival. To my sisters and brother-in-law, and niece and nephews thank you for your love and support. To the many friends, sisters and brothers in the body of Christ who love me and supported me, thank you.

Table of Contents

Foreword by Dr. Izola Wineglass Jones
Introduction
Chapter One
        The Foggy and Confused Place..3
Chapter Two
        Conception..9
Chapter Three
        The Rebellious Years...19
Chapter Four
        Salvation..23
Chapter Five
        Finding Out the Truth..29
Chapter Six
        Getting Help..33
Chapter Seven
        Loving Myself...37
Chapter Eight
        Getting to Know God..43
About the Author

Foreword

The book *Putting the Broken Pieces of My Life Together* tells the story of the effects of emotional, verbal, psychological, physical, and sexual abuse in the life of the author from her childhood through adulthood. The author allows the reader to have an inside look into how the array of abuses impacted the members of her family, particularly her relationship with her mother. The heart-wrenching inner turmoil that an abused child experiences as she tries to make sense of a world that does not value her grabs the reader's attention. Nevertheless, the book shows the power of a relationship with Jesus Christ that moves the author to choose to forgive her abusers, thus giving herself permission to find her voice and to live her life. The courage of the author to tell her story adds hope to this book and provides readers with reasons to believe that healing can be found through Jesus Christ.

– Dr. Izola Wineglass Jones
Licensed Clinical Professional Counselor

Introduction

An aha moment happened to me one morning while I was on my way to work. I was listening to an audio of a speaker sharing his story about his difficult relationship with his father to encourage other people with the same situation. Although his relationship was difficult and strained, God reminded him that he had to honor and respect his father. His words pierced my heart because I was reminded of my own struggle with my mother.

His words opened my heart in understanding, and I realized how wrong I was. I knew that I was angry, but I did not realize that I was failing to honor my mother. My heart felt as if a plumber had opened a clogged drain, and healing was released in my heart. I started weeping uncontrollably for ten to fifteen minutes, releasing the anger and the pain in my heart.

My aha moment did not happen at the most convenient time. By the time I arrived at work, my eyes were red and swollen. My co-workers were looking at me, and I could see their concern written on their faces.

But I had an aha moment that required a commitment! Would I continue to do what I now knew to be wrong, or would I love God and myself and do what was right?

My name is Katelynn Mae. I am a mother of five wonderful, intelligent, beautiful, and handsome adult children. I was living my everyday life and meeting the everyday challenges that life offers. I had reached a major crossroad in my life, and I needed to find the answers to some questions about my life. Some events that had happened in my childhood had left me walking around in a fog—depressed, angry, confused, and sad. I could not understand why I felt this way. I discovered that I was dealing with rejection, abuse, the consequences of rape and many other insecurities in my life. I needed to know the complete truth.

This book shares my journey of how I discovered the truth about myself and what I did with that truth. Dear reader, if you have ever experienced any of these moments in your life, I want you to know there is hope for you. I found hope in facing the truth, finding a solution, and moving forward to greatness in my life, and you can too!

Chapter 1

The Foggy and Confused Place

I know the beginning of my story sounds crazy because it was crazy. I was taking a walk at 4:30 a.m. on a cold, brisk day in February. As I walked in the slushy snow, I was cursing, and trust me, I do not normally curse. I am describing taking a walk, but I was actually stomping through the snow as an outlet to the pent-up anger I felt within. I knew I desperately needed to expel the anger and clear my head.

Without any warning, my mother had kicked my husband, our five children and me out of her house. I wanted to make some sense of her sudden change of heart. We had no place to go, and I simply couldn't understand why she would be so cruel. We had recently relocated from North Carolina to Maryland where she lived. For us to transition to Maryland, we needed a place to stay temporarily so we could save enough money for a place of our own. We had enough money to make the move, so my mother had agreed for us to move in with her while we saved for a deposit and the first month's rent for our own apartment.

We had lived in North Carolina for nearly ten years, and we had decided to return to Maryland so our children could spend more time with their grandmothers. My husband already had a job and was commuting back and forth on the weekends. At the time, moving in with my mother had sounded like a great idea and the answer to our situation. But in the back of my mind, I had entertained some doubts about whether this arrangement would work out. My mother and I did not have a good relationship, and I honestly didn't know if we could stay in the same house and get along.

Even with these concerns, I still asked my mother about moving in, and I was thankful she agreed. My mother and sister were living in her three-bedroom, two-and-a-half bath home, with a family room, a basement, a kitchen, a living room, and a dining room, I thought her house was big enough for everyone to live together comfortably without feeling overly crowded.

My husband and I made sure the seven of us understood and followed my mother's guidelines and instructions for living in her house. We were to keep the house clean with everything in its proper place. My husband and I would alternate days of cooking meals for everyone in the house, including my mother and sister. My family stayed in the basement most of the time to give my mother and my sister their privacy on the main floor of the house.

The living arrangements seemed to work well for a while. I tried to go along with whatever my mother wanted, but I knew disagreeing with her about any matter would present a major problem. We had been living there for almost two months when we inevitably had a disagreement. My sister decided to confront me about that disagreement in front of my entire family. We were all in the basement preparing for the next day of work and school when she got in my face about our mother being so upset.

I could not believe she was behaving the way she was in front of my family. She was overstepping her boundaries, I told her to get out of my face. When she didn't back away or respond, I pushed her away from me. She immediately reacted by punching me, pushing me to the floor, and then pinning me to the floor.

I had no idea that she was drunk and high on marijuana and crack cocaine. My husband and our two sons had to intervene and pull her from me. My mother inevitably heard the commotion and came downstairs to investigate. I tried to calmly explain to her what had happened, but she refused to listen.

Instead, she called the police.

When the police arrived, she informed them that she wanted my family and me out of her house immediately.

The police had no choice but to say, "You and your family will need to leave the premises immediately!"

I could not believe what was happening! We didn't have any place to go at 7:30 in the evening. The only place that I could think of where we could go was an emergency family homeless shelter. My only other option was to call my other sister to ask if we could come and stay with them. All seven of us moved in with my sister, her boyfriend, and my two nephews.

I took my walk in the snow to make sense of why my biological mother could mercilessly kick us out of her house with no place to go to! The chilly walk finally calmed me and helped me think, so I continued my "anger walks" for months afterward. They didn't change the situation, but the walking helped me feel better.

While we were staying with my sister, we tried to move forward with our everyday lives. We tried in vain to pretend that the situation with my mother did not hurt us, but we had been hurt. We were all hurting, and we felt betrayed. Our children were old enough to understand how wrong their grandmother's actions were as well as her reaction and subsequent judgment. They could not understand why their grandmother would kick them out, knowing they had no place to go. I had no explanation for them.

My mother's actions made me want to react with hateful words and even bodily harm, but I remembered the words of my grandmother: honor your mother and father. I remembered a verse of Scripture: "Honor thy mother and father: which is the first commandment with promise; 3That it may be well with thee, and thou mayest live long on the earth" (Ephesians 6:2-3 KJV).

But what about my mother not honoring me! I wondered. Ugh! What I thought didn't matter. I knew I had to learn to accept my mother's actions and somehow find a way to learn how to forgive her. At the time I didn't want to forgive her or even consider forgiving her. I also had to understand that I couldn't change my mother. God is the only One who could change my mother's heart. I eventually came to the reality that if I wanted to be able to live the rest of my life being happy without bitterness, I had to forgive her.

Matthew 18:21, "Then came Peter [one of the disciples] to him [Jesus], and said, Lord, how oft shall my brother sin against me, and I forgive him? Till seven times? Jesus saith unto him, I say not unto thee, Until seven times: but, Until seventy times seven."

This Scripture means that we shouldn't keep track of how many times we need to forgive anyone. When I would think about this situation and many others involving my mother's hurting me, I would find myself angry again. However, as a Christian who has a relationship with God, I knew I had to be honest with my Heavenly Father about the anger festering in my heart. I remember praying, "God, I don't think I can do this thing called forgiveness. I want to confront my mother and retaliate."

Wanting to take revenge is human nature for people who have experienced hurt. God brought other Scriptures to my mind:
Do not take revenge, my friends, but leave room for God's wrath, for it is written: "It is mine to avenge; I will repay," says the Lord (Romans 12:19 NIV).

"Love your enemies and pray for those who persecute you" (Matthew 5:44b NIV).

At some point, I had to decide to do right toward my mother—even if doing so was painful for me. I determined that any time a hateful thought came to mind about my mother, I would go to a private place and pray for her. Let me make this clear: this is not something that I started doing right away. It took me about five to six months before I decided to embark on this path to forgiveness.

Just a side note: not until I decided to pray and forgive my mother did, I start feeling better, and my life started turning around in the right direction. While I was going through this process and living my life, I had to stay away from my mother so that I could heal. I learned that keeping distance between you and someone who is hurting you or disrespecting you—even if that person is your mother—is acceptable. You need time to heal the pain.

I cried my way through the pain. Sometimes my weeping was so intense, I couldn't think straight. I knew I had to find positive ways to release that inner anger. What helped me to release the anger and frustration was to keep a journal, take walks at 4:30 a.m. and work out at a gym. I also went to see a therapist at a Christian Counseling Agency to find help.

My path to forgiveness was a continual process. I followed through with the work and exercises the therapist suggested. I started reading more of God's Word, praying, and venting my thoughts and feelings to friends who would allow me to express them. During my walks, I would pray and ask for God's wisdom concerning everything. I asked Him all kind of questions privately and quietly.

Even then I still had so many unanswered questions about my relationship with my mother. I asked God why these things were happening in my life. I had to surrender to His help in getting through this time of upheaval and misunderstanding. I understood that God wasn't putting my family and me in that unbearable situation; however, I understood that He had lovingly allowed this situation to get my attention.

I needed some understanding so that I would not end up in this situation again. After I was kicked out of my mother's house, my already poor relationship with her disintegrated even more. I couldn't pretend any longer that our relationship was good or even status quo. I had to the face the truth that our relationship had been unstable for years. I knew my mother was angry with me for something other than the decision I had made and the altercation that had taken place in her house.

I desperately wanted to understand why this person called Mother seemed to dislike me so much. I realized, while I was going through this process to gain understanding, that I had a relationship with my mother that I will call a "mommy-daughter relationship." Let me explain what I mean. I felt like I was a child in an adult body, allowing my mother to control and manipulate my life. This scenario has continually appeared at different times throughout my adult life.

I knew the time had come for me to wake up and see the truth. The truth was, not only was I intimidated by my mother, I was also afraid of her. I'm sure you're asking yourself; how can a grown, mature adult daughter be afraid of her mother? I don't know how this can happen in a relationship, but in my situation, my fear was a reality. Pay attention to the key word WAS. There was a lot of hurt, pain, and rejection between my mother and me, and we both needed to heal.

At times I would imagine what it would be like to enjoy a healthy relationship with my mother. In my mind, I visualized being able to talk with each other though not necessarily agreeing with each other—simply conversing with each other. I visualized a relationship of mutual respect for one another when the only relationship we shared was one of disrespect.

I knew that to start having a good and healthy relationship with my mother meant respectfully expressing the truth to her, and hopefully, our relationship would at some point change for the better. I needed to try—even if her response toward me meant our relationship would only worsen. I had allowed my mother to have that kind of control over me because I wanted her love. In fact, I realized I was willing to do whatever was necessary to get her love—even if it meant changing some things about myself.

I know this thinking probably sounds crazy! I do own the fact that changing myself for someone is wrong—even if that person is my mother. But in my journey as I sought to be loved by her, I tried to change to what she wanted me to be.

Chapter Two
My Conception

Nearly everyone can share his or her birth story. The details and circumstances of my story came in bits and pieces after I was a grown adult. I was told by my grandmother that my mother had only been a teenager when she had given birth to me. She explained that my mother did not want to have me.

Hearing that my mother did not want me from my birth was tragic for me to learn. I can only guess that my grandmother felt I needed to know some of the truth about my beginnings. When my grandmother explained that my mother had only been a teenager, I felt that possibly she disliked me because of her young age and the changes my arrival brought into her life. Having me at such a young age probably wasn't easy for my mother.

After my mother gave birth to me in the hospital, we went to live with her parents. A year or two after I was born, my mother found a job and moved into her own apartment and got married. She left me with my grandparents, whom I called Mom and Dad until I was eight years old. They loved me, nurtured me, and cared for me as if I were one of their own children. They had already raised five other children who were now adults and living on their own. Now they were raising me in their household. When my mother would come by to visit me, she would bring me new clothes, shoes, and anything else I needed for school.

When I was eight years old, my mother decided that she wanted me to come and live with her new family—her new husband and my two sisters. My grandparents had to let me go because they had no legal rights or guardianship enabling them to keep me. Since they would no longer be caring for me, they decided to move into a senior citizens' facility near their oldest son who lived in Newark, New Jersey. I could not understand why I could not go live with my grandparents in New Jersey.

When my grandparents moved, I felt like my world had come apart. I felt abandoned by the only two people who really loved and cared for me. Although they had lived in the projects, the years that I spent with my grandparents were secure and safe. They loved me for who I was—their grandchild. When I was sick with allergies and asthma, my grandmother would find the time to take me to the clinic for the medical attention I needed.

My grandparents allowed me to be a child and to have fun. I could go outside and play with the kids in the neighborhood. I played with my cousins who lived around the corner. My cousins would walk me to school and bring me home. In their care, I felt protected and loved.

After I left my grandparents' home to live with my new family, my life was never the same. My world became one of fear, uncertainty, insecurity, sadness, anger, and abuse. Anyone would think that moving in with my mother would be a great opportunity for me to bond with her. Sadly, that did not happen. In fact, when I moved in with my new family, I felt alone and afraid. I cried almost every day and longed for the life I enjoyed with my grandparents.

My day-to-day existence of living in our apartment involved looking out the window, watching the kids have fun outside, listening to Motown playing on the radio, and playing with my two younger sisters. I longed to go outside to play, but I could not. As I look back on those lonely days, perhaps going outside to play would not have been safe for me in that neighborhood. I'm not sure.

I had to adjust to rules in this household that were new to me. I had to change and obey them. When my mother would see me crying, she would call me a crybaby. I didn't like hearing her call me a crybaby, so I decided to stop crying whenever my mother would come around me. I tried to change what my mother did not like about me so she would love and accept me. My only hope of living and existing in this household was to try to do everything and be everything my mother and stepfather wanted me to be. Making them happy became my goal in life.

Living with my new family meant I had to grow up fast and learn how to do tasks I had never had to do before. At eight years old, I had to help take care of my two younger sisters, clean the apartment, learn how to cook, wash the dishes, and take care of a myriad of other tasks my mother and stepfather needed me to do.

I did enjoy having two younger sisters in my life. My six-year-old sister was funny and loved to play house with her stuffed animals. I grew to love them both, but I loved my youngest sister most because she was so sick. When I moved in with my mother, she was four years old though her physical, mental, and cognitive abilities were that of an infant. She had some type of disabling disease that had left her in a paralyzed state. She had little-to-no mobility in her body, though she was able to move her head from side to side and make some sounds. She could not talk or walk.

As she lay in her brown crib every day, I communicated with her by looking into her eyes and talking to her. I would tell her that I loved her. In my heart, I believe she understood me. Although, I was a child myself, my responsibility was to help feed her baby food and change her diapers when I came home from school. I spent all my time with this sister, thinking I could help her to get well and live a longer life.

With life, nothing stays the same, and we eventually moved to a bigger apartment. My disabled sister was given a room separate from my other sister and me. I would go into her room and lie beside her crib on the floor to make sure she didn't feel alone. I also had to help take care of my other sister by looking out for her at school and making sure I walked her home safely every day. After school was over, my sister and I used our key to get into the apartment quietly and went into our room to work on our homework. My stepfather was usually asleep on the couch in the apartment because he worked at night.

On a few occasions when my sister and I came home from school, our stepfather was asleep on the couch near his bar with no clothes on. The first time this happened, I was really shocked to see a grown man naked. Unfortunately, seeing him naked became my new normal.

What I remember most about my stepfather is his anger. Maybe his anger resulted because he was a police officer. He did have some good qualities. He was a good cook, and he especially loved to cook fish every Friday. He also loved to party, drink, and have a good time.

During the day when our mother was not home, he could be unbearable to live with. He would refer to my sister and me as dumb, stupid, and ugly; he would kick us around like we were dogs. He thought picking his nose and chasing us around the apartment to wipe his fingers on us was great fun. His form of play bordered on craziness.

I stayed in my room as much as possible or went outside when I could. Whenever he wasn't playing with us and my mother was out of the apartment, he would call my sister and me into his dimly lit room to take care of his needs. He would ask us to come into his room and massage his back. He would be lying on his bed, wearing only his underwear. As a child, I had never done anything like this. At eight years old, I would massage him from the top of his back to his buttocks. He would then turn over for me to massage his stomach, coming close to his penis and at times touching it.

Doing these massages felt strange to me. Touching a man's private area can stimulate a young girl who doesn't understand what is happening with her body. She soon learns that physical touch can be exciting without knowing that what she is doing is not right. However, I knew I had to obey what he wanted me to do or suffer the consequences.

Living in this household did not allow me to have a voice or express myself. All my feelings and emotions had to stay bottled up inside of me. How does a child learn how to cope in an atmosphere like that? I learned to accept everything as being "normal." I didn't question anything. This behavior continued for a number of years.

As time went by, I began to feel that what I was doing with my stepfather was not right, but who could I tell? Eventually, I stopped going into his room to give him massages. Since I wasn't cooperating with him, he would call my sister into his room to give him a massage. One day I decided to try to protect my sister and stop her from giving him a massage. I don't know where my courage came from. I resolved to go against what our stepfather wanted. When he called my sister to come into his room, I said, "Don't go! Stay here!"

He became angry and confronted me angrily.

"We are not going to do that anymore," I countered.

He came toward me—probably to hit me, so I grabbed a knitting needle to try to protect myself and my sister. What a crazy situation! He could have easily grabbed that knitting needle from me and beat me, but he didn't touch me or hit me. He simply walked away. After that confrontation, the massage sessions stopped.

I never told my mother about what our stepfather had done to us. Although the massage sessions stopped, the results of the molestation and the exposure to sexual abuse would show up years later. Today my stepfather would be considered a pedophile, especially since he was a police officer. When a child has been exposed to any type of sexual abuse and no one is there to protect the child, the door is opened for more abuse in their life.

After I was sexually abused by my stepfather, I was also molested by a classmate in middle school. Her family lived in the same apartment building as our family. I would go to their apartment, thinking that I would get to experience and understand how a real family functioned. I would visit them without telling my mother and stepfather. The family was from Jamaica, so I had a chance to experience Jamaican food and learn a little bit about the Jamaican culture.

One day when I went over to their apartment, my classmate and I were watching television. While were watching a program, she started "wrestling" with me, putting her hands between my legs and on my breasts. At first, I did not really understand how or what was happening, but I recognized the sexual feelings within me were like the feelings that I had experienced with my stepfather.

While we were wrestling, one of her sisters came into the room, and she immediately stopped fondling me. I immediately went home and tried to understand what had happened. Did I initiate her advances? How did this happen to me? Here I was as a young girl being molested again. I knew that what this classmate did was wrong. I never went around her again.

I never told my mother about any of my sexual encounters. I continued to live with the secrets of everything that had happened to me.

Not until I was an adult did, I share what had happened to me of being molested by our stepfather—not with my mother—but with my aunt. I never told my mother because I didn't feel safe sharing anything with her. I felt she would either blame me, not believe me, or have no empathy for what had happened to me.

With all that was happening in the household, I never developed a relationship with my mother. She was only someone who gave me instructions about my responsibilities, and I obeyed her to the best of my ability. Getting a hug from my mother or being told by her that she loved me or that she was proud of me would have been so wonderful. Generally, all I felt from my mother was anger. I wasn't sure if she was angry at something I was doing or had done or if she was just angry with me as a person. This treatment continued throughout my childhood.

One of the outlets that helped me to deal with my home situation was going to school. Some of my teachers at school encouraged me and told me how smart and intelligent I was. I strived for the praise and approval from my teachers by working hard at school.

Another outlet I had was listening to music on the radio, usually songs from Motown. To this day, I love all kinds of music, but Motown is one of my favorites.

I also learned how to become a majorette and use pompoms to perform in the community parades. Classes were offered through our community recreation center. We practiced and learned routines. I was able to participate in community parades during special events. This diversion helped me cope with the continuing abuse in my home life.

When I first moved in with my new family, we were living in a two-bedroom apartment in the Washington, D.C., area. We eventually moved from the two-bedroom to a three-bedroom apartment in Maryland. One morning I woke up to get ready for school and realized something was wrong with my disabled sister. She did not respond to me when I talked to her, and she would not wake up. I knocked on my mother's bedroom door to let her know something was wrong with my sister.

My mother came out of the bedroom and immediately called 911. When the ambulance arrived, the emergency medical technician tried to resuscitate my sister, but she did not respond. While all of this emergency medical care was taking place, my mother told my other sister and me to get ready for school. Get ready for school?! How in the world can I get ready for school when something is wrong with my sister?

In my mind, I did not believe that she was gone. I thought the EMTs would take her to the hospital to help her get better. That was the first time that I had ever experienced the death of someone so close to me. I had been with her every day, helping take care of her. I wanted to stay there to make sure she would be okay. Walking away from my sister whom I had cared for and loved so much to go to school as though everything was okay was brutal. Looking back on that day, I realize now that my youngest sister died not only from a disabling disease but also from child neglect.

Child neglect within a home, within a society and within a community can be caused by a lack of resources to help parents who have little-to-no money to learn about caring for a child who is disabled and to help parents provide for the child's medical needs. Today, thankfully, more resources, more information, and more research and organizations are available to help parents take better care of disabled children.

My mother was unable to get the help and resources she needed to take care of my sister. As a child, when I was faced with my sister's death, I had a difficult time understanding. Although I did not want to leave my sister, I obeyed my mother's instructions, got dressed and went to school. The walk to school felt like the longest walk of my life. Although I was walking with my other sister, I felt so alone. I tried to make it through the day at school as if everything were normal. I cried quietly through that day and for months afterward.

When my sister and I came home from school that day, my sister's crib, clothing, and everything that had been a part of her life was gone. No traces of my beloved sister were left in the apartment.

My mother did not talk to us about my sister's death. To my knowledge there wasn't any discussion about her passing in the household. We did not have any ceremony or funeral for her. It was as if she had never existed. Rather than ask my mother any questions about my sister, I went to my room where I could be away from everyone and cried quietly. I systematically silenced any feelings I had as a child and simply obeyed both my mother and stepfather. I stuffed all my emotions deep down inside of my heart.

In many of the households of my generation, children were to be seen and not heard. My life was an example of that old English proverb. Had you looked at my family life from the outside, it looked great. The apartment was always clean and beautifully decorated. Everything appeared to be perfect and in place—except there were no traces of bonding, communication, expressions of love or emotions. A person looking in from the outside would have been unable to see the difference.

After nine months later, my mother became pregnant and gave birth to a baby girl—a beautiful, happy child who brought much joy to the household. Having some joy and happiness in the family was great, but my sister and I soon discovered the new baby was the favorite of the family. She was the only child who was a product of my mother's marriage. Her birth was a special occasion.

Having a new baby girl did not change the abuse in the household. The mental and physical abuse continued. As the years passed, tension seemed to develop between my mother and stepfather. They started arguing with each other more frequently. His way of dealing with the arguing was to drink alcohol, go to sleep or leave the apartment. During one of their arguments, when he left, my mother chain-locked the door. She gave my sister and me express orders not to open the door.

After a couple of hours, my stepfather came home and tried to get in the door. He called my name to come open the door. I remembered the instructions my mother gave me and did not open the door. Because he was a police office, he knew how to break in the door; after all, he had been trained and that is exactly what he did. When he forced his way in, he immediately came after me, began hitting me and asking, "Why didn't you open the door?"

My mother came out of the back room with one of the wooden bed boards used to hold up a box springs and mattress. When she started hitting him with it, my instincts kicked in. I protected my sisters by grabbing them and running out of the apartment. We hid in the basement of the apartment building. After the fighting was over, my stepfather left the apartment, and my mother yelled outside for my sisters and me to return. Not long after that incident, my mother made some changes in her life, deciding to separate and seek a divorce from our stepfather.

Chapter Three
The Rebellious Years

After going through all the craziness, I endured as a young child, I became a rebellious and angry teenager—for good reason. I hated my stepfather for molesting me and exposing me to a world of sexuality. After all, he was supposed to be the protector of his family. I started to act out at home, at school and toward my mother. My mother did not understand what was happening to me. She could not help me or show me any love or acceptance during this time. I did not care about myself or what other people thought about me. I had taken care of everyone else in the house, but no one was looking out for me emotionally.

Don't get me wrong. My mother was taking care of my physical needs for food, shelter, and clothing. I believe she did the best she could. She did not realize I was hurting, and I never told her. During my teenage years I blamed myself for the absence of my biological father, I blamed myself for my mother's dislike, and I blamed myself for my stepfather's molestation. I thought something was wrong with me. Indeed, something was wrong; I needed help! I had grown up in an environment of abuse.

I started looking for someone to show me love and acceptance, and I looked for it in all the wrong places. I started hanging out with the wrong crowd and became very promiscuous and smoked marijuana. Over the years, my life spiraled down from bad to worse. I continued to take care of my sisters and babysit for my cousins as well. I longed to be loved, valued, appreciated, and validated by the people who were closest to me. Unfortunately, that desire was never fulfilled.

In my searching and seeking for what I thought was love, I began having sex. I quickly discovered that having sex with a man does not make you feel loved. I became pregnant on two different occasions, thinking a pregnancy would bring me the love of a man. I then discovered that having a baby does not ensure the love of a man.

I decided to get an abortion with both pregnancies, though the thought of an abortion was frightening. The first time and second time I became pregnant, I was still a minor. I searched for a clinic in the Yellow Pages to find a location where I could get the abortion without my mother's consent. Back then, having an abortion cost between $200 and $300. Because I had started working at the age of 14, I had been able to save up a little money and had enough to pay for each abortion.

When I found a clinic, I made an appointment and took the bus to the clinic. When I walked inside, I noticed the place was set up like any other doctor's office. I wrote my name on a list for the receptionist and waited for my name to be called. When she called my name, she directed me to a counseling area where everything that was involved with having an abortion was explained in detail. I was given a complete understanding of what would take place before, during and after the abortion. I was even offered other alternatives to having an abortion—carrying the child to full term and then giving up the child for adoption or carrying the child, giving birth, and living in a home for unwed mothers.

I made the decision to go ahead with the abortion because I knew I could not take care of a child. I was only a child myself, and I knew I needed help—let alone care for another child. Where were my feelings and emotions during this time? I was scared—but not scared enough not to go through with it. Even though I felt dreadfully alone, I was used to handling things on my own. I was also used to hiding and pushing away any of my feelings and emotions. I sat stoically listening to the counselor give me instructions for the abortion.

She directed me to a room to prepare for the surgical procedure. The doctor and a nurse explained what type of precautionary measures I needed to take after the procedure. The doctor provided an antibiotic to help me with the healing process. He explained that I needed to get proper rest. He also explained that I needed to have a follow-up appointment with a gynecologist to perform a routine D&C to make sure that everything had been safely removed. A D&C, which is a dilation and curettage, refers to the dilation of the cervix and the surgical removal of part of the lining of the uterus and/or contents of the uterus by scraping and scooping. This therapeutic gynecological procedure is most often used during a first trimester miscarriage or an abortion.

I remember lying on the table and thinking of all the things that could go wrong because of what I was doing. I was scared, alone, and sad. I felt sad because I really love children yet here, I was aborting not just one child but eventually two. I decided to go through with my plan even though I knew taking a life was wrong.

The doctor came into the room with a tray containing a long needle. I felt the pressure and pain of the needle going inside of me to numb the area. I felt a second needle injecting a chemical solution to kill the fetus. I could not believe that I was going forward with this procedure. What else was I going to do? I was praying that God could forgive me for what I was about to do. Although I wanted to cry, I held in the tears so that I could focus on what was happening. After that procedure was done, I heard the sound of a machine.

The machine was used to suck the unborn fetus out of my uterus. Once the procedure was completed, I was allowed to rest for a short time to make sure I was not going to hemorrhage or go into shock. After about 30 to 45 minutes of observation, the doctor gave me a prescription for pain and an antibiotic to take for 30 days. I walked out of the clinic and took the bus home.

Taking the bus for transportation can be challenging but riding the bus home after undergoing an abortion was even more agonizing. Not only was I dealing with the physical pain of the surgery, but I was also dealing with great emotional pain. I cried all the way home while trying not to make a huge scene on the bus. I made it through the bus ride home.

When I arrived at home, I told my sisters and my mother that I was not feeling well to explain why I was not at work and staying home. The physical part of the procedure was over, but the emotional torment and the guilt I experienced would continue for years after the abortion. I started having nightmares in my sleep, visualizing the doctor's inserting the needle and waking up in a cold sweat. All types of negative thoughts about the details of the procedure, about what I had done and blaming myself constantly bombarded my mind. I had thoughts of God's never forgiving me for what I had done. I made it through that difficult time only by the grace of God.

I was living in a cycle of abuse that needed to stop. I started using marijuana and drinking alcohol to try to numb the pain of what I had done. I begin to hate myself and my life. I felt I was plummeting into a deep pit. I reached the point of desperation, wanting and needing help.

Looking back over that time of my life, I realize I would never find love in anything or in anyone else because I first needed to find the love of God. In loving God, I would be able to love myself and others. God is love, and everything about Him represents the love that anyone needs.

Chapter Four
Salvation

When I was living with my mother and sisters, I was partying and going to clubs with a male friend who lived in the neighborhood. His mother attended church, and her church was hosting a concert called "Living Proof." My friend's mother asked me if I would like to attend the concert, and she gave me a free ticket. The concert was scheduled for July, in 1981. I thought I was going to a concert like any other concert prepared to have a good time drinking and getting high. I went to this concert and discovered that this concert was different. There were Christians in the entertainment industry.

At that time, I didn't know what a Christian was, so let me explain what a Christian is. A Christian is anyone who has experienced a spiritual new birth by receiving Jesus Christ into his or her life. These Christian entertainers came together to share their testimonies about their relationship with God. The concert was held at RFK Stadium in Washington, D.C. Each person shared his or her personal experience and relationship with God and how becoming a Christian had changed his or her life.

As I mentioned, I attended this concert just as I would any other club or party, expecting to have fun getting to know people, getting high and continuing my usual self-destructive pattern. As soon as I stepped inside of the arena, I could feel something different. I did not know what it was, but the atmosphere felt different. There was singing, dancing, praising, and testifying. It wasn't the typical stuff that I was used to experiencing at a concert. I simply listened and watched.

A host came to the stage to address the audience, and he welcomed everyone to the concert. He explained that the purpose of the event was for Christians to gather together to exalt God. He also explained how sin had entered the world through Adam and Eve and how sin separated mankind from God. In order to reconcile man back to God, He sent His Son Jesus to die on the cross so that we can be reconciled to Him. He explained what salvation was about and started talking about how Jesus came to earth to die on the cross so everyone could receive the gift of salvation. He also explained how Jesus loves and cares about everyone and that He will love and accept you just as you are.

I did not understand everything they were talking about, nor did I understand what was going on, but I listened to find out more. After the speaker started talking about Jesus, I felt something different. I now know I was feeling the presence of God. Once the presence of God came in and encircled the stadium, I felt like the heart of everyone there had been touched, including mine! I began to cry.

I felt like someone had unplugged a flood of pain and emotions inside of me. I was crying uncontrollably and really could not stop. Looking back, I realize that God was working on my heart, releasing so many years of pain. Attending that concert was the beginning of my healing process. I continued to listen to the speaker as much as I could. With all the crying I was doing, I could not hear every word being spoken.

What I did hear repeatedly was that Jesus loves me and accepts me just the way I am. I needed and wanted that type of love so much. The speaker then went on to share how everyone can have this love by receiving Christ as their Savior and by asking Him to come into their heart and save them from sin. All I had to do was to receive this gift from God. What I needed to do sounded simple enough, but I wondered, how could it be that simple when everything else in my life is so hard. I simply could not believe that accepting Christ as my personal Savior could be that easy.

The speaker then invited everyone interested in receiving Jesus Christ into their heart to come down the stairs to the bottom of the stadium. Counselors were waiting who could tell us more about Jesus and how to receive Him into our hearts. I still did not quite understand what accepting Him meant, but at that moment, I decided going forward was worth finding out more.

How I had longed for someone to love me and accept me as I am—with all my mistakes and flaws. I walked down the stairs and spoke to one of the counselors so I could have a better understanding of what being a Christian was all about and how this could happen for me. While I was walking down the stadium stairs, I was still crying. As a matter of fact, I could not stop crying. One of the counselors gave me some Kleenex and a booklet that provided more of an explanation of who Jesus is and why He became a Savior for all of humanity.

When the counselor asked me if I wanted to receive Jesus into my heart, I said yes. I needed and wanted to be saved from all the sin I had created in my life. The counselor prayed with me and led me in saying the sinner's prayer.

Romans 10:9-10 (KJV) says, "That if thou shalt confess with thy mouth the Lord Jesus, and shalt believe in thine heart that God hath raised him [Jesus] from the dead, thou shalt be saved. 10For with the heart man believeth unto righteousness; and with the mouth confession is made unto salvation."

I acknowledged that I understood that I was a sinner, and I believed that Jesus died on the cross for me so that I could be reconciled to God. After I prayed that prayer, I cried even more. I am convinced that, at that concert, God was working in my heart and healing me of so many years of hurt and pain.

The counselor shared how important it was for me to find a Bible-teaching church to attend so that I could learn more about my relationship with God and the Word of God so I could continue to grow as a Christian. I had no idea what church I should attend because this Christian walk was all so new to me. I knew I did not understand a lot of what was said. The counselor prayed with me and asked God to help me find a church.

After the concert was over, I went home and thought about everything that had happened to me at that concert. I shared my testimony with my mother and my sisters, telling them that I had received Jesus Christ as my personal Savior into my heart. "I became a Christian."

Their response was a look on each face that said, what has she gotten herself into now?

I told them that my salvation was a real experience, and Jesus Christ was real. I continued to go through my day.

The next step I took in my Christian walk was to find a church to attend. I remembered the name of the church that my friend's mother attended and decided to visit to see what it was all about. I went there that Sunday and continued attending for about six months before I became a member. I wanted to make sure I understood what being a Christian meant for me.

SEEKING FORGIVENESS

After I became a Christian, my life began to change. God was helping me to deal with the issues that I had carried in my heart for so many years. I had to deal with the hurt, the pain, the rejection, the abuse and all the troubles in my life. First, I dealt with the hatred I had for my stepfather and the anger I had toward my mother. The question that you are probably asking is "What if they were the ones who caused the pain?"

My friend, it doesn't matter who caused the hurt. My responsibility was to forgive those who had hurt me so that I can be forgiven myself. I strongly felt that my responsibility was to forgive my stepfather and my mother. I dealt with the anger I had toward my stepfather first. I knew I had to forgive him for molesting me and being so abusive to me as a child. I wrote a long letter to him, expressing how much I had hated him for how he had treated me. I basically told him the truth on paper. But at the end of the letter, I also asked him to forgive me for hating him. I told him in the letter that I had forgiven him for what he had done to me. I was also able to share my new knowledge about Jesus Christ and the wonderful change Jesus had made in my life. I expressed to him that I hoped and prayed that he would get his life together and give his life to Jesus.

My letter was about four-to-five pages in length, and I gave it him when

I saw him. I did not see him again for a couple of months. When I saw him again at a convenience store, all he said to me was that he had read my letter. I was shocked that he did not have any other response. The nerve of him, right?! He never responded to the molestation with an apology nor acknowledged that he had abused me.

Although, I did not get the kind of response I had wanted from him, I knew I had done the right thing; I was so glad I had forgiven him. I forgave him for my peace—not for him. Doing what I felt God wanted me to do made me feel so much better and so much freer. After I saw him at the convenience store, I would cross paths with him on rare occasions.

Three years went by. One day my family shared the news that our stepfather had been found dead inside his taxicab. I could not believe it. I was so grateful that I had obeyed God by forgiving one of the persons who had hurt me. I had no idea that he would be gone shortly after I gave him my letter of forgiveness. I thank God I had the opportunity to confront my abuser and make it right for myself.

I would not suggest to anyone to confront their abuser. Seek advice if you were involved in an aggressive situation. You can forgive the perpetrator(s) who have caused hurt or harm in your private time with God. You can write a letter to the person like I did and express your true feelings, then shred it.

As I mentioned, I was also seeking God's help to deal with the anger I had in my heart toward my mother. After I forgave my stepfather, the process of forgiving became a little easier for me. Before I explain what, I went through to forgive my mother, I want to say that I am thankful my mother raised me and took care of me to the best of her ability. For some reason, my mother held a strong dislike toward me, and I could never understand why. Her animosity seemed to surface more and more as the years went by, distancing us even more.

One evening, I went into my mother's room where she was watching the television. I asked her if I could talk with her and again explained to her how I had become a Christian. I wanted her to better understand why I was asking her to forgive me. I explained to her how being a Christian had changed my life. "God has healed my heart of much hurt and pain." Then I shared that I had hate in my heart toward her. "Please forgive me for hating you."

I can't quite remember my mother's response, but I don't think it was a good response—probably because she didn't understand why. At that moment God immediately released the pain and anger I had in my heart. Just saying those words helped me to love my mother whether or not she continued to reject me. I was hoping the truth I shared with my mother would help her to be able to love me back. Unfortunately, I was wrong!

I wanted to believe that my mother loved me, and I do believe she probably does loves me in her own way. For healing to take place in our relationship, we both needed to be honest with each other and begin to develop a new relationship. At this point in my life, I realize my mother was doing the best that she could in loving me, raising me, and taking care of me. For that, I am very grateful. Even though I was an adult, my mother still seemed to expect to have the same type of control over my life she had had when I was a child. I am trying to apply what is in the Word of God about honoring and respecting my mother and father that my days may be long upon the earth. This Scripture is so true. I do respect my mother; I simply don't understand why she has harbored such a dislike toward me. Because of that antagonism, I learned that sometimes we must forgive over and over again.

Chapter Five

Finding Out the Truth

Both my mother and stepfather wanted me to believe that my stepfather was my biological father. Before my parents divorced, my stepfather had adopted me. I had never believed in my heart that he was my biological father. First, I looked nothing like him. And secondly, I thought it was really weird that my stepfather would molest his own child.

When I was in my late 30s and talking with my mother on the phone, she decided to share the circumstances of my conception. Judging by the annoyed anger in my mother's voice, I sensed she did not really want to talk to me about this matter. She finally acknowledged that when she was very young, she had been raped by my biological father. In shock, I listened carefully to what she said. Once she told her story, she quickly ended the conversation.

The next day my mother called me back and told me what she had shared wasn't true. I felt in my heart that she had told me the truth, but I needed to know for sure. I had been lied to so often, I simply didn't know what to believe. I decided to call my aunt and ask her. My aunt confirmed the truth of my mother's violation. She explained that the attack on my mother had happened at a party she had attended with her older brother and sisters.

Wow! What?! I could not believe what I was hearing. After I talked to my aunt, I felt like someone had snatched a rug from underneath me, and I was lying flat on the floor, desperately trying to figure out what had happened and gather my thoughts. Now I understood why my mother had such a strong dislike toward me and the seething anger she seemingly held inside. I finally understood why my mother had mistreated me the way she had for most of my life.

I had so many light-bulb moments and flashes of understanding. I finally understood why my mother's facial expressions changed whenever she saw me. When I came to visit her for a gathering or an event, I watched her whole demeanor change. I look just like my mother, and whenever she sees me, I have no doubt I am a constant reminder to her of what my birth father did to her. I have no doubt her response toward me is based on that horrible act.

This knowledge also explains the reaction I got whenever I tried to ask my mother questions about my father. I finally heard the truth, and I felt numb. I think I was feeling numb in part because there was no chance, I would ever meet him or even want to because of the circumstances of what happened to my mother. I have since learned that he is deceased, so meeting him will never be an issue.

My mother also told me that my biological father has a daughter and a couple of sons. How can I meet this family when he raped my mother?! I have a half-sister and two half-brothers?! To me, meeting them would create an awkward situation at best.

So many emotions and thoughts went through my mind that day. I felt anger, sadness, disbelief, denial, and confusion among others. I felt that I was going through a grieving process, but I wondered, how could that be? No one has died.

I felt confusion because I was an adult and just now hearing the truth about my life. Even knowing this truth does not take away the pain that I felt from my mother all those years. I also feel my mother responds to me as though she thinks I would cause her bodily harm because my father did. That supposition is so far from the truth. I have tried to be and do what my mother wanted most of my life so that she would love me. I can do nothing else except pray that God will help her know the truth about me. In knowing the truth, perhaps one day she will be able to love me unconditionally.

I am not saying that I no longer have moments when I struggle with anger toward her. At those times, I have humbly gone to her to ask for her forgiveness. I have let her know that there will still be times when I get angry, but I want her to know that because I am human, I am working on it—whether or not she is working on her anger. I must be responsible for taking care of my part, which is doing what is right so that I can heal myself and continue to be blessed.

Truthfully, I am grateful to be alive! My mother could have aborted me the way I aborted two children. My mother did the best she could to raise me despite living with the pain of her rape. I have realized that for my mother to give me the affirmation that a daughter looks for from her mother is probably not possible. My mother can only give me the pain of what she has had to deal with in the past and what she is still dealing with in the present.

Being sexually abused—assaulted, molested, raped—is a terrible violation that no girl, teenager, or woman should ever have to experience. Rape is a crime, typically committed by a man (or a woman), of forcing another person to have sexual intercourse against his or her will. This crime, which strips the victim of everything, leaves the person trying to rebuild and heal while living life with the pain and hurt of the violation.

Going back to the conversation I had with my aunt, I asked her if anyone in the family tried to get my mother any type of therapy or counseling. For such a traumatic experience, anyone would need it. My aunt replied, "No." From the way my mother's life is turning out, I can see that she did not get any type of help. I pray for my mother, and I hope that one day her heart will heal and that she will seek the professional help she needs to enjoy her life. Since I have gone to therapy and I have forgiven my mother, I am able to love her and accept her the way she is. It has become so much easier for me to love her.

Chapter Six

Getting Help

At this point in writing this book, I finally knew the details of why my mother may have a challenging time of loving me. I am one of the consequences of her rape. I believe when my mother sees me, she remembers the violent crime perpetrated against her as a young girl. I realized that my stepfather had molested me for many years. My story as a child seems like some type of crime drama. As I made mention, other incidents of molestation also took place in my life.

I know that other young children have experienced and are experiencing worse situations than what I endured. Though I was happy to finally know the truth about my life, I was also bitterly angry. I was angry with God because I thought He should have protected me. I was angry with myself for feeling like I should have done something about the molestation. I was angry with my mother for directing her anger toward me for what my father did. I wanted to stay angry because I felt that I had rights, and what had happened to me wasn't fair.

I finally came to realize that blaming anyone including myself is needless. Life happens, and what happened to me wasn't God's fault. I was blaming Him for not being there when, in fact, He was there throughout my entire life. I believe and know that He is the One who protected me and kept me through the craziness of my youth. My life could have ended up much worse than it was.

I understood that God doesn't control the decisions that our mothers, fathers, and stepfathers make in their lives; He allows them the free will to make their choices. It would be great if we took the time to ask God for the guidance and wisdom that we need to make decisions. Life would be so much easier.

We only seem to turn to Him for His help when a serious situation like a health crisis arises or when we are being confronted with death or when our backs are against the wall, and we don't know what to do. We may not even ask for His help then. I am unapologetically making many references to God in my book because without Him, I would not have survived my childhood. I would have been in some type of mental institution without Him.

The next step I took in caring for myself was to seek therapeutic help. I took the time to find a therapist who helped me to understand my situation better and to get a different perspective on how to resolve what happened. Nothing is wrong with accepting therapeutic help. Don't be afraid to see a therapist. Have the courage to seek the help you need to resolve these issues for yourself.

I checked with my health insurance company to see if expenses relating to therapy were covered and found that counseling sessions were. Then I searched for a Christian therapist and found one. I had a co-pay fee each time I made a monthly appointment to see my therapist.

The therapist guided me through the labyrinth of issues that had clouded my mind for years. Doing all the work and the exercises the therapist suggested helped me tremendously. After seeing the therapist, I also started doing what I call "forgiveness work." In my private time with God and/or my devotional time, I would write down the names of the many people in my life who had ever hurt, wronged me, or offended me. I knew I need to find forgiveness for these people, so I began writing their names as God brought them to mind. Beside each name, I wrote what the person had done that hurt or offended me. After I recorded everything, I called each person's name out loud and declared that I had forgiven him or her for the painful situations each had a part of creating in my life. Then I would pray and ask God to bless them if they were still alive. Then I would write a new truth about the circumstance or situation in my life. This practice freed me of the hurt and pain I was unnecessarily carrying with me through life. By the time I finished my list, I had nearly 30 pages of names and offenses. Thank You, Lord, for freeing me!

Because of all the hurt and pain I experienced as a child, seeing myself as the victim would have been very easy. Thinking that I would never break these destructive cycles in my life would have also been easy. My new truth is that I am a strong, courageous woman because of what I am overcoming. The cycles are being broken because I have chosen to deal with the truth and to find the help I need.

Another new truth I have embraced is that, despite my past, I deserve the best of everything that God has for me.
Philippians 2:12-13 (KJV), "Wherefore, my beloved, as ye have always obeyed, not as in my presence only, but now much more in my absence, work out your own salvation with fear and trembling; 13For it is God which worketh in you both to will and to do of his good pleasure."

I had to learn how to work out my own salvation and to get the healing and help I needed. Learning how to work out my own salvation does not mean that God is not there to help me. He is. I've had to do my part to get the help and to do the work to receive healing. He is there to help me and guide me in this process and to heal my heart's pain. Going to a therapist gave me the opportunity to understand the basics in life—like understanding the roles of my parents in my life. I also came to understand what a family unit is all about. Although my family was not a support base for me, I was blessed to get to know people who encouraged me and shared their wisdom with me while I went through this process. Their encouragement helped me to remember I have so much to be thankful for now.

Many years ago, I shared some of my story with an elderly woman at the church I attend. I was sharing about the difficulty I was having with my mother and not understanding my relationship with her. She responded that, in due time, God would reveal the truth to me when I was ready to handle it. Although my mother still faces challenging times of loving me and accepting me unconditionally; I am reminded of an uplifting Scripture: Psalm 27:10 says, "When my father and mother forsake me, then the LORD will take me up." I embrace the fact that my Heavenly Father loves me unconditionally. Knowing that God loves me helps me to be able to love my mother unconditionally. I have learned not to look to my mother for nurturing or validation. Even though that sounds harsh, cold, and indifferent, I know my mother cannot give me what she doesn't have to give me. She was hurt by the violent crime of rape. She only remembers the pain of the situation. She couldn't give me what I needed as a child and what I need as her adult daughter. I have had to learn to look to God and friends to love me.

Chapter Seven
Loving Myself

One of the last challenges I faced on my journey of life was to learn how to love myself. That mandate from God sounds easy for someone else to do, but for me, I found following His directive very difficult. I felt like I was running in a marathon with hurdles and mountains to climb to reach a place where I felt like I was at peace with myself and all that had happened. I finally realized it is what it is. I now understand why my mother feels the way she does toward me.

In my youth, I internalized the pain and blamed myself for the anger she was feeling. I had convinced myself something had to be wrong with me, which resulted in moments of depression, intense sadness, and despair. That is now the past. As I continue to learn who I am, a new script is being rewritten about me. I now understand and embrace the fact that God has created me and made me in His likeness and image. He knows all about my life.

I also continue to take every positive step I know to take, like going to therapy to help me in my journey to victorious Christian living. One of the books that my therapist suggested I read is entitled, Free Yourself from Painful Memories, Reclaiming Your Inner Child by Ken Parker. This book has been so helpful in the healing process that I am still using the principles I gleaned from its pages. I continue to journal and to exercise.

I was doing well until the day I became curious again. I wanted to ask my mother some unanswered questions that were still swirling in my mind. I decided to call her and ask her if we could meet, and I told her why. We scheduled a Saturday so that we could eat together. When we arrived at the restaurant, something inside of me said, "Don't do this. She is too fragile to deal with any of the pain of the past!" I don't know where this thought came from, but I listened to the nudging. I did not ask her any questions. I simply enjoyed her company as much as I could.

The next day I was angry again, and I thought I had been doing so well. This time when my anger surfaced again, I cried out to God. "Please, God," I begged, "help me to heal from this anger and from the pain I still feel." Even though I sound crazy, I had really decided that I needed another mother—someone different. I had failed to remember that healing is a process, and everyone's process is different.

Without counting the future cost, I started looking for someone else to be the mother in my life that I did not have. I did not realize this seeking for a substitute was risky for so many reasons and predominantly for the following two:

• My search for a substitute revealed that I had still not forgiven my mother.

• I was refusing to accept God's choice for my mother.

In my heart, I knew my thinking was wrong, but I continued my search. And just like God, the help that I needed showed up in a way that I did not expect.

Our church invites guest speakers to come and share their stories. Sometimes these stories can really help you when you need it the most. On this particular Sunday, the guest speaker was sharing how God has divine protocols and systems put in place for our lives to help us to live successfully on earth and to grow as a Christian.

I looked up the word protocol to give me a better understanding of the word. I found that protocol is a system of rules that explains the correct conduct and procedures to follow on formal and informal occasions. The guest speaker shared how he had a difficult relationship with his father. When he made that statement, he had my undivided attention because I was and had been having a difficult relationship with my mother. I completely understood where he was coming from. He had grown up in a household with a father whose practices went against what he knew to be right. He shared different examples of how difficult it was to obey his father and his rules. But God, in His wisdom, reminded him that although his father was falling short with practicing things that went against what he knew to be right, he still had to honor his father.

I could not believe what I was hearing. He shared the different times during his childhood when he tried to take matters into his own hands by disobeying and disrespecting his father and trying to change what his father was doing behind his back. In every situation God reminded him not to try to take charge of the circumstances. He repented, went to his father, and asked for his forgiveness.

God has principles and precepts in place for Christians as well as anyone else. We must follow the Fourth Commandment: "Honor thy father and thy mother: that thy days may be long upon the land which the LORD thy God giveth thee" (Exodus 20:12 KJV). We must follow this directive even if our parents do wrong and cause any type of harm or pain in our lives. This speaker shared how he had followed through with what God told him to do each time. He also shared how his siblings did not honor their father while he was alive. They felt justified in showing him great disrespect. In later years, when their father died, so did the siblings.

The words of this man's testimony really pierced my heart, and I felt as if God was speaking to me directly through this man's relationship with his father. My relationship with my mother paralleled this preacher's experiences. After I heard his testimony, I felt as if someone had removed a plug from my heart that released the anger in my heart. I started weeping uncontrollably for at least 10 to 15 minutes.

The crying for me was good even if the timing was inconvenient. I was on my way to work, and when I arrived, my eyes were red and swollen. I could tell that my co-workers were wondering what had happened to me. I didn't explain to anyone but went about my normal routine. Then the most profound thing happened at work. My supervisor asked, can I help you with what is bothering you?" "Thank you. I appreciate your concern, but no."

He simply stood there, apparently pondering how he could help me in my obvious distress. He walked into his office and came out carrying a framed picture. He showed me the picture and said, "This is a picture of my mother. I had an extremely difficult relationship with her. She never accepted me. I tried to love her the best way I knew how. Toward the end of her life, she was finally able to be at peace with me and accept me." I thanked him for sharing that story with me. I could not believe I was witnessing God's using my supervisor to encourage me. How I thanked God for that amazing experience. It was amazing because the supervisor had no idea what I was struggling with. His story about his mother encouraged me.

Moving forward, I knew the time had come for me to deal with me and how I feel about me. Psalm 139:14 (NKJV) says, "I will praise You, for I am fearfully and wonderfully made; marvelous are Your works, and that my soul knows very well." I began thanking God for my life. I thanked Him for bringing me through the abuse of my childhood and youth in my right mind. I thanked Him for who I am and declared, "I love myself."

Everything about God is beautiful and wonderful. Although I had experienced some damage in my life, I realized it is possible for anyone to be healed and repaired. The time had come for my mind and heart to get the memo and understand this truth. I had to do the work! I had to learn how to rebuild my self-image and confidence. I studied the Bible to understand what God thinks of me.

When I rise in the mornings, I thank God that I am alive. I look in the mirror, and I speak affirmations about myself. I have to understand that no matter what happens in my life, God loves me unconditionally with all my faults, and sins. Jeremiah 1:5a (KJV), "Before I formed thee in the belly, I knew thee...."

Regardless of the circumstances of my life, He knew that I would be conceived out of rape. When God created us, He created us with great qualities. We need to learn what those qualities are and develop them and learn how to enjoy our lives and start fulfilling our lives with purpose. I am reminded of a precious Scripture in Jeremiah: "For I know the thoughts that I think toward you, saith the LORD, thoughts of peace, and not of evil, but to give you an expected end" (29:11 KJV). God has such love for me and for anyone who wants to receive it. That kind of love makes me committed to living my life so that He is pleased with me.

This relationship I have with God has taught me how to love myself and to fight for myself. Every time negative thoughts and words come up about myself, I fight against them and speak a new truth about myself with either the Word of God or with a new truth I have discovered.
Such as:

- "I am a child of God" (Romans 8:16 KJV)
- I'm an overcomer
- "Be strong in the Lord and in the power of His might" (Ephesians 6:10 KJV)
- "And he said unto me, My grace is sufficient for thee: for my strength is made perfect in weakness" (2 Corinthians 12:9 KJV)
- "Not to think of himself more highly than he ought to think; but to think soberly, according as God hath dealt to every man the measure of faith." (Romans 12:3 KJV)

The relationship I have with my mother is better. It's can become strained and difficult at times. It was so strained that I decided to take a break from my mother. I left from being around her and my sisters for about two years. I was at peace and enjoying my life. God in His infinite grace doesn't allow us to stay in situation or things that need to be changed for long. In my personal time with God, I told him that if my mother ever needed me for help, I would be there to help her. Well, the next day, I received a phone call from one of my sisters stating that my mother was in the hospital. Can they get my help to take care of her. I told her that I would be happy to help. God, you really have a sense of humor to bring me back in connection with my mother so quickly after I offered my help. I was back into my mother's life once again. This time it was different because I was different. I greeted her in the hospital. She greeted me back and thanked me for coming back to help her. I was there to care for her alternating days with my sisters. Sometimes we stayed overnight to care for her. I did not mind. I had two years to clear my head and be at peace with myself. Our relationship went well in the beginning. A situation came up and those same thoughts and feelings would come back to plague my mother's mind. Which meant that she had a flash back and instead of seeing me, she remembered the pain of what she experienced from my father. She started yelling and demanding that I leave out of her place. I was told that my services are no longer needed. Gee, this situation seems familiar. I've experience this before with her. I would love to tell you that I was not in my feelings when that happened. That's not true. The old thoughts and emotions came to the surface. I had to do the forgiveness work all over again. In my private time with the Lord, I repented of any negative response I wanted to have towards my mother, and I declared that I forgive her whether she is angry or not angry. I prayed for her. This time it did not take me as long to come out of it. After this episode, it took my mother a few days to realize how wrong she was. A doctor's appointment came up and she needed me to give her a ride there. She texted me and asked me if I could drive her to the appointment. She apologized. We continued to interact with each other as if nothing ever happened. I am learning how to love her the way I want to be loved—without expecting anything in return. I am at a place in my life now where I can look back and thank God for the process and the journey—though it was and still is a challenge at times.

Chapter Eight

Getting to Know God

I trust that God has used the story of my journey to encourage you. I hope you were able to receive some helps to make some new changes in your life. If you have read this book, and you are interested in receiving Jesus Christ as your Savior, let me share the help I received on my journey. You need to know the following:

1. God's plan for you is to live and to have peace. The Bible says, "For God so loved the world that he gave his one and only Son [Jesus Christ], that whoever believes in him shall not perish but have eternal life" (John 3:16 NIV).

2. Humanity's problem is separation from God. Being at peace with God is not automatic because, by nature, human beings are separated from God. Humankind has tried to bridge this separation in many ways without success. The Bible says, "For all have sinned and fall short of the glory of God" (Romans 3:23 NIV).

3. God's solution is the cross. God's love bridges the gap of separation between God and humanity. When Jesus Christ died on the cross and rose from the grave, He paid the penalty for our sins. In the Bible, Jesus Christ says, "I am the way and the truth and the life. No one comes to the Father except through Me" (John 14:6 NIV).

4. Our response is to receive Jesus Christ as our Savior. God invites us to respond to His love by crossing the bridge through trusting Jesus Christ. This means accepting Christ's death on the cross as payment for our personal

sins and receiving Him as our Lord and Savior. The Bible says, "To all who did receive him [Jesus Christ], to those who believed in his name, he gave the right to become children of God" (John 1:12 NIV).

"If you confess with your mouth, 'Jesus is Lord,' and believe in your heart that God raised him from the dead, you will be saved" (Romans 10:9 NIV).

God invites everyone to repent (turn away from your sins), and by faith receive Jesus Christ into your heart and life. Some people can attend church and accept Him into their heart. But some people have not had that opportunity. I had the opportunity to pray the sinner's prayer while I was attending the concert at RFK Stadium that I have already mentioned. You can talk to God yourself wherever you are and pray this prayer to Him. You don't have to be in church. He will hear you, and He would like to be your Father and guide your life.

What to pray:

Heavenly Father, I know I am a sinner. Right now, I repent and turn away from my sins. I believe Jesus Christ died for my sins, rose from the grave, and is alive today. I open up my heart and life to You. Jesus, I ask You to come into my heart and save me from my sins and become Lord over my life. Saying this prayer and meaning it is only the beginning step. When you pray this prayer, He will hear it immediately!

Some of the next steps you will want to follow include:

1. Learn more about being a Christian by reading and studying the Word of God. You should start by getting your own Bible. Find a version that helps you to understand along with the King James Version so that you can study them together. Reading the gospels of Matthew, Mark, Luke, and John are helpful to see the mind of Christ. The Bible, which is God's love letter to us, contains His guidelines for living a victorious life. After you get your Bible, pray, and ask God to open up the mind to understand the word, and to guide you and help you understand His Word.

2. Ask God to show you a Bible-believing church to attend and to help

you grow in your faith.

    3. After God directs you to a church to learn more about growing your relationship with Him, you will need to get baptized. Baptism will not save you; baptism is your way to identify with Christ.

    4. Make a commitment to follow Jesus Christ—no matter what happens in your life. He loves you just the way you are, and He will help you change. Remember that change is a process! Ask Him for guidance and direction about everything. You will be surprised how He wants to help you learn to love you.

About the Author

Katrina Royster is an author, missionary, and entrepreneur, who's passion is to encourage others and help them to identify if there is something in their life that needs to change. Her goal is to help others to think differently and to reach a different level in their life. Katrina's future goal is to travel, and to share her story and faith with others. Katrina resides in the Washington DC Metropolitan Area.

KATRINAROYSTER.COM

www.ingramcontent.com/pod-product-compliance
Lightning Source LLC
Chambersburg PA
CBHW071845290426
44109CB00017B/1926